A New Way To Invest

7 Proven Steps to Get
Rich before you Retire

Jim Jorgensen
Radio talk show host / author

Cover Design and formatting by: Laura Shinn
www.laurashinn.com

The paper edition of this book is available at special quantity discounts to use as gifts or for use in corporate training programs.

Call Special Sales Manager at 925-209-7442 or e-mail jim@financialsavvy.com

While a great deal of care has been made to provide accurate and current information, the ideas, suggestions, general principals and conclusions presented in this text are subject to local, state and federal laws and regulations, court cases and any revisions. The reader is thus urged to consult legal counsel regarding any points of law – this publication should not be used as a substitute for competent legal advice.

Other books by Jim Jorgensen

The Graying of America
Your Retirement Income
Stay Ahead in the Money Game
How to Make IRAs Work For You
Money Lessons for a Lifetime
It's Never Too Late to Get Rich

Dedicated to:
My wife, Nancy Jorgensen
who taught me everything
I know about life.

A New Way to Invest reveals simple steps and profound truths on how you can change the way you invest. With small regular contributions you can build wealth and peace of mind when you retire. Jim's thirty years in the market and on the radio make this a rare book that can be read and understood by anyone who wants to retire rich. Start on the journey now with these well-tested insights for life.

Praise for Jim Jorgensen's book

Bill Groody, Formally NBC News, Washington

"Your new book is an articulate expression of your long standing investment strategy which has served you through good markets and bad."

Bill Donoghue, America's mutual fund guru, author of Rebuilding America's Wealth.

"Whether you have a lot of money or just a little, whether you are just getting started investing or nearing retirement, this book is immediate financial salvation that works for everybody."

Contents

Introduction

Once upon a time in a city somewhere in America lived a hard-working employee who used his experience and felt comfortable solving the daily problems. But he felt the money he was pouring into his retirement plan was going nowhere. He also realized he could no longer understand what was happening to his money invested by some people in a far away land. And he often felt helpless while he watched much of his previous payroll contributions disappear.

He began to understand if he wanted to build a realistic retirement nest egg he would have to take responsibility for his own actions and make his investment decisions. In short, he could no longer wait for good things to happen. It was time to trust his ability to solve his own money problems.

What had taken him so long to come to this conclusion was not that his plan was continually losing money, but that he knew he'd have to spend the time to remain constantly alert to recognize the buy and sell signals to protect his assets. And he'd also have to learn a new system of handling his money. It was time he continued to tell himself he didn't have. But now it became apparent that he had to find the time if he wanted to retire with enough money to pay his bills, play golf and plan the vacations he'd always wanted.

He found himself looking over a maze of investment plans but most of them were too complicated and required too much time. They also required other people's help which he now felt he could no longer trust. What he needed, he told himself, was a plan where he could watch over just a few socks and spend maybe 15 minutes a week to stay on top of his game. Then he discovered Trend Investing and if he was faithful to the weekly drill he was convinced he could do as well as others using this plan. At least it was worth a try; his current mutual fund program had been a bust, never making much money in an up and down market and costing him a lot of fees and expenses.

With the discovery of Trend Investing came a spring in his step. At last he knew what to do to lock in profits in an up and down stock market instead of waiting for a phone call to help him that never came.

In my 35 years of advising investors and from letters and callers on my nationally syndicated radio shows, I've witnessed scared and confused investors watch their retirement plans lose money beyond their control. I've felt their pain from opening mutual fund statements and with glazed over eyes looking at what's left of their once hefty IRA or 401(k).

I've also found most investors don't take advantage of the ups and downs in the stock market to make double-digit returns each year. They feel frozen in panic when the bottom appears to be dropping out of their investments and miss the stock market rebound.

But knowing how to invest your money is only half the game. That's because, after you have a plan to become rich you have to want to become rich. You have to be willing to work the plan and no matter how difficult it becomes, never give up. I remember a 74-year old man who made the 240-mile trip to visit his 80-year old brother, who was ill, driving his lawn mower all the way. He chose his John Deere riding mower as his vehicle because he didn't have a driver's license. Hitched to the back of the mower was a trailer in which he hauled supplies and camping equipment. He averaged only five miles an hour and the trip took six days.

What I discovered talking to people on the air and at seminars, along with the man on the lawn mower, if you want to become wealthy and you stick with your plan, you can. The problem is most people underestimate what they can do with a plan and a few bucks a day. They look at the money they have and think becoming rich at retirement is beyond their reach.

"But Jim," I heard the caller on the radio say, "I only have a couple thousand to invest and it won't make any difference anyway."

Don't laugh. You've probably said this before. Almost everyone has. But it's not true. There are a lot of distractions as we plow through life, but I'm reminded of a story of a man who in spite of a meager income saved a few dollars each day. He never missed the few bucks stashed in the cookie jar, and today he's retired with a hefty income and money in the bank. But I'll never forget what he told me about the secret of how he saved his money.

"I don't buy things because I have money; I buy things because I need them."

Like many of the richest people in America he began at age 25 investing $200 a month in good stocks and continued to do this until he reached age 65. Over this 40-year period with $200 a month he'd invested a total of $96,000, yet his retirement nest egg had grown to more than $1 million. He told me what surprised him was *he made most of his money over the years on the growth of the money he'd already invested.*

A listener in Chicago called my radio show and said he had a simple way to understand how he got rich with very little money. "Try to visualize it this way," he began. "To make a loaf of bread you let the dough rise. The bread gets bigger over time. You don't do anything; the yeast makes it rise. That's the same way your money grows in your IRA, but instead of yeast, it's the incredible power of compounding over time."

Remember, as you read this book; hide some money each month in the cookie jar where you put your spare cash. If its $200 a month and you start now you could retire rich. Of course, like everything else, the more money in the jar each month the bigger the payoff at retirement.

The good news is that the principles of building wealth on a shoe string have remained the same since the guy rode his lawn mower. But the stock market and the way we invest changed dramatically in the 2000s, compared to the roaring 1990s. Investors in the 90s started to think the annual 20 percent gains from Standard & Poor's 500 Index funds were their constitutional right and that making money in stocks was easy.

But the bubble bursting stock market in early 2000 and the recession starting in 2007 have been a very different story indeed. A continuing unfolding of one major corporate scandal after another has severely shaken investor confidence in the whole system of investing. All of the major institutions that were supposed to protect investors—the corporate board of directors, auditors, accountants, stock analysts, investment bankers, stock exchanges, attorneys general, state and federal securities regulators—all failed to uncover or stop massive fraud and shareholder abuse by a laundry list of American corporations including Enron, Adelphia, Qwest, WorldCom and many others.

But the decade of the 2000's told us one thing: In uncertain times its best to invest in the common stock of some of the nation's big blue-chip companies with long established well-known brands, and a long history of profits.

The purpose of this book is to outline my investment strategy that has made money in up and down stock markets for years. If you put these rules into practice and into your life, you can end up a far richer, more comfortable investor than the vast majority of Americans who are still hiding their investments under that proverbial rock.

Step 1:
Save Some Cash

It may sound crazy, but it's true. You have to have spare cash to invest in the stock market. I learned that early in life talking to the farmers at the farm equipment store where my dad was keeping books. As was my custom, and with a wink at my dad, I reached into the five-cent Coke tub, dipped my hand into the ice water, and took out a bottle.

The farmers were talking about the new hay rakes and money. I drew closer to listen to their words, not because I was interest in anything about hay rakes but because I knew these farmers always had money. And money in my youth was a precious commodity. It was easy to tell the farmers from the salesmen, the farmers wore bib overalls. Not just any overalls, the garment of choice, as far as I could tell, had the logo "Oshkosh B Gosh" sewn on the top flap. As you might guess, it didn't take long for a high school kid who wanted to become rich to wear the Oshkosh B Gosh label.

Farmers are a strange bunch. You pretend to be comfortable with them, but you never are. They know it, but they also pretend they don't. But much of what I learned in life came from talking with the farmers.

If I had to wrap up all the financial planning ideas in the world they could be boiled down to one simple premise told to me over a hay rake: First, save some money, and then spend the rest. Everyone in town knew it worked for the farmers; they paid cash and drove Cadillac's.

I was on roll now so I went for the good stuff. "If I'm not too personal," I said, "how did you learn to pay yourself first."

"The problem most people face is they can't save any money because no one has sent them a bill. To get started I made up a bunch of bills, put them in envelopes addressed to me, and gave them to a friend. Each month he dropped one in the mail and I paid the bill. And now," he said with a smile, "I can pay cash for everything."

At the time I didn't have much money, but from talking with the farmers I knew I had a head start on most people accumulating wealth. Later we lived near a golf course with a pond and I quickly made the tools of my trade: a long handle net to scrap the balls off the bottom of the pond and back in our basement I built a wooden slide lined with brushes powered by a garden hose. With my homework, trips to the pond and work in our basement I was a busy guy. But in high school it paid better than a paper route and I learned that after some holidays the pond was full of golf balls and I had a real payday. At $2.50 a box the stray polished golf balls piled up the money and when my passbook account when to double digits I started buying stocks. I didn't know much about Wall Street, but from pulling my wagon full of groceries home with my mom I knew the names of my favorite drink Coca Cola, the people who built my electric fan General Electric and the Pepsodent toothpaste my mom required

I used each day. I figured that was a good place to start. If they were in my house they must be in other people's homes. Later I learned all of these companies had well-established consumer named brands and people would pay extra for the comfort of knowing they had the "real thing."

When I went to the university driving my golf ball paid for convertible, I learned that business professors never talked to the farmers, never drove Cadillac's, and saved only a few dollars a month instead of creating investment portfolios. Maybe that's why none of them taught courses on getting rich. I learned how to accomplish that from the farmers.

But today Wall Street appears turned upside down. In fact, after the last decade with a stock market crashing one day and standing still the next, you probably feel like Howard Beale in the 1976 film *Network* when he says: "I'm mad as hell, and I'm not going to take it anymore."

You're mad because your broker or financial planner told you to buy Enron, Washington Mutual, Lehman Brothers or some computer stock set to double in price because they were making huge profits.

You're mad because you later lost your money when the profits turned out to be nothing more than a classic case of cooking the books. You're mad because the rush into mortgage debt was said to be as safe as cash and turned out to be almost worthless. And you're mad because analysts on Wall Street made millions of dollars while they told investors to buy new issue stocks they privately ridiculed. All the while you were glued to the doom and gloom each day as the stocks and funds continued to slide. Like a caller on the air told me, "the stock market shock feels like a guy in a bath tub holding a toaster – and in this plunging market no one knows when to let go!"

More likely your past investment statements have been tucked into a file box unopened while you stuck you head under the covers and followed the once time-tested buy-and-hold approach to investing. But now, in 2010, you can buy a share of Citigroup – the nation's largest bank – that sold for $55 at the beginning of 2007 for $4. Or, for the price of a single spark plug you can buy a share of General Motors stock.

Like most investors, in this prolonged period of a crashing stock market, you probably avoided making any changes in the way you manage money. Instead, you waited for the stocks or mutual funds to regain their value. History tells us, however, when you stand pat things could get worse and they usually do.

But is fear and denial the best way to manage your financial future? Not if you want to build a sizeable nest egg for your retirement years. In fact, this book is about ways to encourage you to make a commitment to change the way you invest in the future.

As you survey the smoking wreckage of your IRA and 401(k), you probably wonder: *What should I do now?* My answer is start with Rule #1.

Rule #1

The secret to prosperity is your
ability and desire to adopt changes
in the way you manage your money.

If the recent market turmoil hasn't frightened you, if you're not ready to take charge of your own investments, then I want you to consider *Time* magazine's January 28, 2002 cover issue that told investors: "With so many choices and no one to trust in today's world, **you're on your own, baby.**"

The article asked: "Can I count on my broker? Who's looking after my 401(K)? What's happening to my mutual funds in my employer retirement plan?" *Time* concluded that the old safety nets are gone. And it really is true: You're on your own baby!

But if you can change what you *believe,* you can change what *you do.* As a result, the first thing you need to believe is that like *Time* magazine you're on your own and you have to manage your money. I'm not going to claim to know everything about investing – I only know what has worked for me (and what hasn't) over the years. A wise man once said, "If you want to know how you feel about someone, talk about their youth." So let me tell you a little about mine.

I was born in Omaha, Nebraska in the 1930's and grew up in a household that today would be called economically disadvantaged. I didn't know that at the time, but I did know since my family didn't own a car, and if I wanted to go someplace, I walked. And when I went to a birthday party I had to bring a gift. My mom usually bought the gift, but one day she gave me a dollar to buy one. "What can I buy?" I asked. She said, "Buy whatever you'd like, I'm sure Johnny will like it, too." I went to the store and found just what I'd always wanted. All I had to do was convince my mom to let me keep it. I tried the ploy that Johnny might not like it and maybe we should get another gift. Mom didn't buy that. Then I said it had batteries and maybe we should open the' package to make sure they were still good. Mom said we'd trust the batteries. I even tried to get sick the day of the birthday party in the hope that Mom would forget about the gift.

Do you know what it's like to give a birthday gift that you've always wanted to someone else? That's the whole deal with birthday parties, except I never forgot that day and I vowed that someday I'd learn how to make enough money in the stock market to buy the things I wanted.

I was able to do that by investing early in some of the items each week in my wagon from the grocery store. Buying and holding stock in these household names has, over the past 40 years, made a lot of money. How much? $100 invested back then, or as I like to say the equivalent of forty boxes of golf balls, could be worth about a half a million dollars today.

But as I entered Wall Street a new world opened up for me. The traders on the floor of the Exchange told me about buying on the dip and selling on the curve. This concept became Trend Investing. In other words, the trend of the share price indicated when you buy or sell a stock. But to make this work you have to become an active manager of your investments.

That's what I've tried to incorporate in this book and help you learn the difference between people who actively save and manage their money and those who don't, and those who make money in up markets and don't lose the same money in down markets.

The importance of this plan became clear, even to those who never look at their mutual fund statements, when the stock market wiped out 40, even 50 percent of their retirement nest egg in a recent major business turndown.

I gave early pre-publication copies of this book to my employees and to those who listened to my radio show because I was eager to explain ways to bring success in their financial lives and, for the first time, imagine themselves managing their own money.

Money is often the soul of our well-being. We pursue it each workday because we believe it will make us happy. But if we get it and then lose it, we can face a traumatic future. If we get it, keep it and make it grow, it can lead us to a full and rewarding life with the people we love.

Over the years one of the most important things you can do in life is to make yourself happy, to share your love and understanding with your family, and to take each day one day at a time. After all, your trip to financial success should be as much fun as arriving at the destination.

What I've learned investing in the financial markets, on Wall Street, writing six books on personal finance and listening to thousands of callers on the radio is what you'll read in this book. It's also my belief that if you save some money each month and invest in good stocks the results can literally be the difference between retiring rich and working behind a fast-food counter.

I hope each time you read this book you'll find something new and useful for yourself, your loved ones and your friends. I'm glad that I can share what I've learned and I wish you well as you build your financial future.

Step 2:
Stay Out Of The Same Old Rut

Maybe you're stuck in a comfortable rut that you've followed for years. As long as things haven't fallen completely apart, why make a change? It reminds me of an Aesop fable. The hares think they can do better if they're constantly on the move, always looking for the new investment or selling an old one that went into the dumpster as they race towards the finish line.

The tortoises believe they don't need to zig or zag; instead they hold on to what they have, ignore the stock market and believe they are making steady progress toward a goal. If the going gets rough and the stock market makes an occasional hair-raising drive they pull into their shell. In the dark, they wait for their investments to recover.

Today, most people who contribute to a retirement plan at work like a 401(k) behave like tortoises. How do I know this?

According to a recent study by the University of Michigan, looking at a group of 1.2 million workers in more than 1,500 retirement plans, found that fully 80 percent of workers initiated no trades in their 401(k) plans during a two-year period. Eleven percent made only a single trade.

The findings are even more alarming when you consider that many large 401(k) plans permit employees to sell stock on a daily basis.

The one fact that should now have become obvious: if you want to make money over time in the stock market you're going to have to find someone to look after your money. That someone might not be a mutual fund manager, a salesperson disguised as a financial planner, not an investment advisor at the bank, or not a local friend.

Today that someone is you!

In fact, the chances are you may have depended on others without realizing that no one really cares about your money as much as you do. Ask yourself - did any one call on your sinking mutual funds? Did you learn about the plummeting Washington Mutual, Lehman Brothers and Citicorp stock before it went into the dumpster? Did anyone offer to sell your investments in the recent stock market plunge and save what you had left?

You may also realize that stuck in a rut you no longer leap for the letter opener when the mail brings your investment statements. You seldom look up the value of your portfolio. What was once a vague sense of fear about the future has transformed itself into unmistakable terror that your financial world could collapse at any time.

When you look over your mutual fund statements what kind of mood are you in? What do you *want* to see in those statements? Do you sense that you are torn between letting things go to the next statement just to see if things get better, or take charge, pick up the phone and try something different?

The 15-minute drill with the gang

On a Saturday morning at Starbucks, as was my custom, I had coffee with the gang. We talked about last week's golf game and about how many of our friends were losing money in the hot picks that floated around the office.

"Look at the guy that lives next door," a member of the group in workout clothes said. "He's worked for the same company for fifteen years and after socking all that money into his 401(k) and IRAs he tells me each year the overall balance inches up if it moves at all. He said it feels like he's dropping dollar bills in front of his lawn mower," he said with a grin.

"The problem with this guy, as we've all learned on Saturday morning," I heard from across the table, "is that everyone has to cope with unexpected changes. They can make life complicated, even challenging, but if you resist change because it's new or unfamiliar you can be taken by surprise and find that most of what you want out of life is no longer within your reach."

"I hear you," another said. "He's just stuck in the same old rut. Now let's get down to business and compare our 15 Minute Drills," he said, laying his newspaper on the table. "What do you have you have to sell and keep?"

Everyone marked up their paper checking the movement of their mutual funds and stocks and a feeling of accomplishment spread across their face. The buys that morning were going to make some members in this group a lot of money. They were using the cash they saved from their previous sales to buy the stock at the bottom of the curve. Then with the 15 minutes a week drill they could concentrate on when to later sell the same stock at the top of the curve. The purpose of the weekly meetings is to make the stock market work for the investor. That's important because of Rule #2.

Rule #2

History has shown the biggest
risk is not being in the
market when it rises.

[30]

How do I know this? Because over a period of time more than 90 percent of the gain in the stock market can occur in just a few days. The Bull Market from 1983 to 1987 is a good example. Those investors who panic and sell on a downturn and were out of the market the best 40 days in the five-year period [that's 40 days in 1,825 days] had an average annual total return with dividends of just 4.3 percent.

That's why I say if you're out of the stock market when it rises from a sharp downturn you'll kill any chance of building a realist retirement nest egg. Unfortunately, this news has been lost on most investors. Here's why. During a market meltdown, frozen in fear as their stocks and funds plunge in value and locked in place, they miss the selling opportunity to take their profits off the table. But that's one of the secret of making money in an up and down market.

Rule #3

The stock market goes up and down.

In March, 2009 with the Dow Jones Industrial Averages around 6,500 and giant financial firms on Wall Street collapsing like dominoes, smart investors knew that the economy would rebound as it has in all previous stock market melt downs.

They also knew that stocks like Ford, Goldman Sachs and Bank of America were, according to the Federal Reserve, too big to fail. With an economic recovery it was only a matter of time until these stock prices climbed once again.

Rule #4

The best time to buy a stock is
when no one wants to buy; the
best time to sell is when
everyone wants to buy.

Or, as Warren Buffett, another sage investor from Omaha says, "you should be fearful when everyone else is buying, and buying where everyone else is fearful."

I remember very well March, 2009. I was speaking to a national convention in San Diego and some lady, with concern across her face, asked "Do you expect the Dow Jones Industrial Average to fall below 6,000?"

I replied, "Not if it's recently been 10,000. Until the market shakes out its fears, this is a buying opportunity before it comes back to its previous high."

As I expected, in March of 2010 the Dow Jones Industrial Averages were once again over 11,000. That's a hefty 70 percent gain in about one year from a market low to a market high. During a rollercoaster stock market like this it's important to remember rule #5.

Rule #5

The key to building a nest egg today is making money in an up market and avoid losing that same money in a down market.

By using Trend Investing, here's what I did when the stock market hit bottom:

In March, 2009 I bought 200 shares of Ford and Bank of America and 100 shares of Goldman Sachs common stock. My 15-

minute weekly drill told me their stock was starting to creep back up. But more than that I figured:

Since **Ford** did not take any government money on the financial bailout and because they had a good product line and a credit line for their dealers to sell cars, Ford should make money as the economic recovery continued.

Since **Bank of America**, one of the largest banks in the country, had branches all across America with billions of deposits the government could not let the company fail. I also knew the bank had a massive stream of income from millions of customers each month that would eventually pull the company back into the black.

Since **Goldman Sachs** had lost its main competitors Lehman Brothers and Bear Stearns, they were about to sit on a money machine on Wall Street. In good financial shape, they were in an excellent position to grab huge chunks of the business and profits would soar as the economy recovered.

Therefore, I invested $8,312 in March, 2009.

Buy price: As of March, 2010
Ford $1.80 to $12.00
Bank of America $3.76 to $18.00
Goldman Sachs $72.00 to $175.00

Let's say you had
invested in these stocks.

From an initial investment of $8,312, I had a year-end account value of $23,500. That's a gain of $15,188 in one year.

But that's not the end of the story...

As you will learn in this book, Trend Investing is a long-term way to manage money and build wealth. And buying on the dip and waiting for the economic recovery also takes time.

Now, with glazed over eyes, consider what this total return could be in four years. In 2008, Bank of America's stock sold for $50 a share, Goldman Sachs', $225 a share.

Assuming the economic recovery continues and the stocks return to these former share prices, here's what my portfolio might look like in 2011 or 2012:

Ford: $12.00 to $2,400
Bank of America: $50.00 to $10,000
Goldman Sachs: $225.00 to $22,500
Total portfolio value: $34,900

From a purchase price in March, 2009 of $8,312 my persistence in following Trend Investing as outlined in this book could result in a profit of $26,588 in 2012. No guarantees, but I've always bet on the nation's economic recovery from a downturn and I've never been wrong.

A New Way To Invest

Step 3:
Know When To Fold

If Cinderella were dancing on Wall Street many investors might think the clock never strikes midnight. That their investment can always wait for the carriage ride back to a profit. But apparently most investors never met Cinderella at the ball. She was racing for a disappearing carriage; they are waiting for a disappearing investment.

So you see Wall Street is really like the ball with Cinderella when her gown turned into rags at midnight. You're stocks can also turn into rags if you fail to pull the trigger before midnight.

Make no mistake, to be a successful investor you'll need the determination and guts to quickly buy and sell your securities. I know cutting losses can be emotionally tough. That's because most people understand buying a stock or mutual fund is much easier than selling one. To buy you only need the basic optimism that the stock will go up and create wealth.

Sometimes the tip comes from a friend, sometimes from some investment newsletter, and often at a party or from someone who heard the tip at work. But once the investment goes sour it's tough to sell and admit you were wrong. That's hard for many people to do.

But the big problem to overcome is the typical decision not to pull the trigger until you've recouped all your losses. But history tells us once a stock goes into the dumper the stock market doesn't care if you made or lost money. And what you paid is not important and has no bearing what investors will pay in the future. You have to accept the fact that what's gone is gone. Just because you've lost a substantial sum doesn't mean your luck will change.

The trick is to realize when your fund or stock has fallen 5 percent from its recent high to sell before the "whales" – the big mutual funds and pension managers – dump the same stock. They can't unload their huge holdings over night, and in fact many money-managers continue to tell investors the stock is doing well, while desperately placing sell orders and watching the price decline.

Let me say again, once the stock is trending down, once you're weekly 15-minute drill tells you to sell and take profits or cut your losses, you have to act like a cold-blooded vampire because, unless you manage your own money, a mutual fund is not going to call you and tell you its fund is going into the tank. Nor is it likely that a broker or financial planner will pick up the phone and give you the bad news. As *Time* magazine has already told us, we're in a world of do-it-yourself investing.

You're on your own baby!

Managing your money can be a new game and it can often be a numbers game. And the numbers start as soon as you invest. But, as you'll find out in this book, the numbers go against the stand patters who can lose two ways even if they later break even.

Let's say you had $20,000 in a mutual fund, but when you got your last statement the fund was worth only $10,000. Your palms are clammy and your heart is pounding as you look at what's left of your account and think about the hair-raising dive in the stock market. If you're like most people what's really running through your mind is how to save what's left of your nest egg. In fact, you probably don't care if you make any money; all you want now is to break even.

But consider this: If you lose money and you want to break even the next year you'll have to make a huge profit just to get back to where you where before you lost the money.

Consider these grim numbers:

One-year loss - Gain to break even

25% loss requires 33% gain
50% loss requires 100% gain
75% loss requires 300% gain

[40]

And I've got more bad news you're not going to like. Let's look at making the money you lost back. If you could earn 9 percent a year on the money you lost and avoid paying taxes and other fees, it could take you eight years to re-build your loss of $10,000 and turn your IRA or 401(k) back into $20,000. *That's eight years wasted building a retirement nest egg.*

But if you avoided the loss in the first place with the weekly drill, and earned 9 percent each year for eight years on the money, your investment account could now total $40,000 instead of $20,000.

Under this example, once you've made up the loss, is the huge difference in your retirement nest egg at age 65. If you are 35 when you lost 50 percent in one year, and you make back the money in eight years, here's the numbers:

Investment: $10,000 $20,000

First 8 years: 20,000 40,000

At age 65: 205,000 410,000

In this case you lost twice!

Once when the value of the fund was cut in half.

Once when you failed to make any money on the money you lost until you retire.

Take this quiz.

Which would you rather do for the next two years?

Invest in a mutual fund with an 80 percent return one year and a 50 percent loss the next.

Invest is a 5 percent savings account.

My guess is you'd pick the fund that made an 80 percent return, and say, "*let's go for it!*"

But, my friend, you're looking at the screaming headline for a mutual fund with a huge loss the previous year. With a $10,000 investment in a stock or fund that's earning 80 percent return the first year, you'd have an account balance of $18,000.

But with a 50 percent loss in the second year, the account balance falls to $9,000. With the same $10,000 investment in a five percent savings account, the total of the account at the end of two years could be over $11,000.

Now be honest. If you picked the high-flying mutual fund you never thought it could cost you more than you would earn in a laid back insured savings account. Right? Of course not.

But then you probably believed with an 80 percent gain this was just the fund to make money and not follow the last high-flyer which you watched go into the dumpster.

Let's look at some actual examples of picking mutual funds based on their recent short-term track record.

In 2009 Aegis Value stock fund was a top-performing fund with a 93 percent return, according to investment research firm Morningstar. This record came on the heels of a dismal 2008 when the fund lost 51 percent and fell near the bottom of its category.

How did investors do?

2008 invest $10,000, lost 51%, year-end $4,900

2009 gained 93%, year-end $9,957

Birmiwal Oasis, a small-cap growth fund, turned in a 91 percent gain in 2009. But in the previous year it lost 63 percent.

How did investors do?

2008 invest $10,000, fund lost 63 percent, year-end $3,700

2009 gained 91% year-end $7,067.

That's why Rule #6 is so important.

Rule #6

Investors can lose more money
when share prices fall than they
make when share prices rise.

That empty feeling of losing money may have happened to you in the past, but I know someone who has an answer: Warren Buffett, the most famous investor in America. He puts first things first.

Rule Number 1: *Don't Lose Money.* When someone asked him what was Rule Number 2, Buffett simply said,

Rule Number 2: Don't Forget Rule Number 1

Sometime we can't see the obvious because we can't see the future from where we stand in the present. Think again of the hard-earned money you've lost in the market that won't be there when you retire. Say you lost just $5,000 last year. In 25 years, when you apply for Social Security, that five grand could have been $50,000 resting in your IRA.

Then think about the money you could have made on the money you lost over the last twenty-five years. Money you could have used for a great vacation instead of counting Social Security checks.

Let's be honest, Warren Buffett is on to something when he says don't lose money in the market. In fact, I believe this is the really big factor in building your future financial life.

You only have to look at 2008 to see how Buffett's rule comes into play. According to Lipper, who has been tracking stock mutual fund performance records since 1959, if you had $100,000 in your 401(k) plan at the start of that year, you've lost $40,000 by the end of the year.

But the full effect of Buffett's rule becomes clear when you consider you'll have to earn a 66 percent return in the next year on your new balance of $60,000 just to get your account back to where it was a year earlier. What if you can't beat the experts on the Street and earn a 66 percent on your 401(k) assets in one year? If you can earn an average annual return of 9 percent you'll need an additional 6 years to turn the $60,000 back into $100,000. Another painful lesson for investors is that under this example you just lost 6 years of earning a return on your original 401(k) money.

Let's use the $40,000 loss in this example and say you have about 25 years until you collect Social Security. You're probably wondering what it costs to lose this money because you sat on your hands and were afraid to do anything. If you can earn an average 9 percent annual return until you collect Social Security, the $40,000 you lost could amount to a cool $350,000 when you hit retirement age.

The scary part: on average, each year over that 25-year period, your average annual return on that initial $40,000 you lost could be $14,000 a year! As I was told on the floor of the New York Stock Exchange, an average annual return of 35 percent can make you rich!

Let me explain it this way. Every dollar you lose in the market this year could be ten dollars you won't have at retirement. That's why I say on radio and television if you have any money to invest, no matter how much or how little, this compounding principle can still work for you. Here's why...

80 to 90 percent of the money
that ends up in your retirement
nest egg could be money you never
saved or invested at all.

Rule of 72

[47]

But the clincher in building a retirement nest egg might be how much you actually earn on the money you've invested. No one talks about this, but it's the secret of becoming rich.

There's a simple way to determine how fast your money can accumulate over time and make you rich. It's called the Rule of 72. This rule lets you quickly determine approximately how many years it will take an investment to double in value if the rate of return remains the same.

For example, if you want to double your money in 7 years, divide 72 by 7 and you get 10.3. Your money has to earn 10.3 percent a year for the next 7 years in order to double.

If you want to double your money in 6 years, divide 72 by 6 and you get 12. Your money has to earn 12 percent a year for 6 years to double your money.

But playing it safe with a 5 percent savings account, you'd have to wait almost 15 years to double your money. And with a one-year insured CD paying maybe 3 percent you could wait 24 years to double your money. Over time these numbers add up.

Suppose you start with $10,000

A 3 percent annual return over 25 years could grow to about $18,000.
A 5 percent annual return over 25 years could grow to about 32,250.
A 10 percent annual return over 25 years might total $100,000.
A 15 percent annual return could be worth about $325,000.

You might not earn 15 percent a year in common stocks and funds, but staying in savings accounts at a lower annual rate of return can make a huge difference in your retirement nest egg. Fortunately for me and my kids, the lightning bolt hit home when I discovered that I might be able to double my money every 7 years in the stock market.

Let me show you again the effects of low returns over time on building a retirement nest egg.

A one-time deposit of $10,000

15-yrs or 30-yrs
Savings 5%: $20,000 or $43,000
Stocks 10%: $41,700 or $175,000

Look at this way. Once you know the rule of 72 you begin to understand how important the percentage of your annual return over time can be. As I've said, the other important point is the magic of compounding, with only a few dollars a day you can build a sizeable retirement nest egg.

Step 4:
Work On Your Investment Plan

The mythological Greek figure Sisyphus was condemned to Hades with the fate of repeatedly rolling a huge stone up a hill only to have it roll down again each time. Even more mythological than Sisyphus is the notion that you can build a retirement nest egg over many years and not look out for the stone rolling your way.

From my own conversations with people at seminars and on the air I can tell, like Sisyphus, there are millions of people who don't know what they've invested in and why every time they look around a huge stone have flattened their investments. If you want to avoid the rolling stone, now is the time to develop your own personal investment plan.

Successful investors usually start out with companies they understand. In these companies, they look for the right opportunity on the basis of the realization that the product is a well established brand in the consumer's mind and sales volume and profits will continue to grow. In that case, you swing for the fence.

You remember my wagon I lugged back from the grocery store. Well, as I've said, my golf ball money from scraping the pond went into stocks that had a lock on the consumer. With every washed and scrubbed golf ball I could sell I bought Pepsodent because people brush their teeth every day, Coke because people get thirsty, KB Homes because people want and need to buy homes and later in life Starbuck because people have a habit of drinking coffee.

In each case the product or sales of the company is tied directly to the cash register – the more or less consumers buy directly affect the profits of the company and therefore the price of the common stock.

Here's how Trend Investing works:

The first step:

Find out what you have. As a caller on the air told me, "Until you know what you've got you don't know what to do." I agree. Unfortunately, too many investors almost never look at their holdings and have no idea what has happened to their stocks and mutual funds.

Here's what you can do:

Buy the Saturday *New York Times, Wall Street Journal* or other paper with the stock and fund tables. As you move to the web, replace the newspapers with www.bigcharts.com. You can also list your stocks and funds on your brokerage web site. This page will automatically keep track of your stocks and funds each time you go to the web site. On this web site simply type in the name or ticker symbol of the stock or mutual fund and the site will display the history over the last one to five years. The graph gives you a good idea of how and when the price of the security rose or fell. If the chart tells you the stock or fund has been in a downward slide, or is five percent less than its recent high or your purchase price, you should cut your losses and sell.

One way to look at a possible sale of the stock or fund is to ask yourself *would the stock or fund be worth buying at today's prices?* If the answer is no, and you'd rather not buy more, sell. Put the money in your Lock Box.

Once you've decided to sell and cut your losses you have another decision: dump all at once, or sell gradually? My experience tells me if the stock has been a loser, is one you wouldn't buy, dump it all. If you have a fear of missing out on a rebound my history of looking at the stock market tells me the odds are slim to none you'll make money later on with a loser.

The second step:

Find a stock that will directly benefit from an up tick in consumer spending and an upbeat economy. You're only interested in the effect of an economic downturn or upturn on the company's business. The first indication could be when consumers slow down spending.

Again, Starbucks Coffee comes to mind. At the start of 2007 I held 100 shares of Starbuck stock at $35 a share. But as the economy went into a deeper slump and jobs were disappearing at a fast pace, I read where people were backing off buying Starbuck lattés at $4 plus. I visited the local stores, talked to the staff and learned the news reports were true. Thinking that sales would continue to decline and profits would take a major hit as people avoided the pricey coffee, I sold the stock from my 15-minute weekly drill after a 5 percent decline at $33.25 a share.

The stock could always take a leap upward after I sold, but as I've learned on Wall Street it's better to cut your losses on a stock you want to sell before the next downturn. Anyway, I put the sale of 100 shares, or $3,325, into my cash Lock Box.

Watching the stock each week I found that I was right. By October 2008, with the slowdown at the coffee counter, the stock had fallen to $10.50 a share. But I stayed on the sidelines in a down market. The economy wasn't getting any better and my visit to the coffee shop told me that business had again slowed and the shares had fallen to $9.60. That was good enough for me. My weekly drill told me that the stock had started an up tick, and with the money in the Lock Box from the recent sale of Starbuck stock, I was in a perfect position to buy back the stock. I converted the cash into 346 shares of stock. The important point is that my original investment was the same, only the number of shares had changed from 100 to 346.

Then Starbucks closed hundreds of store, cut overhead, and came out with an instant coffee they guaranteed was as good a ground coffee. Better yet, for stockholders the company sold instant packages at Target and Costco. So, as the economy recovered and people return to their habit of rushing back into the coffee shops, I will was one happy guy. By the start of 2010 Starbuck stock was $23 a share. By May it was $27 a share. Instead of sitting on my hands with an account of 100 shares worth $2,700, I held 346 shares worth $9,342 – all because of the weekly drill, watching the economic recovery, and in the case of

Starbucks, the return of the habit of drinking coffee. Believe me, ten grand never tasted sweeter!

The Powerful Kicker

But that's only the beginning of the good news. What most investors don't realize is the future gains from making money in an up market. The powerful kicker that could let you tour Europe in retirement is the nest egg building that could occur in the future.

My feeling is by 2011 Starbuck's stock could at least return to its former price, or $35 a share. Now I'm in the chips, making money like I did when I walked the floor of the New York Stock Exchange because now the numbers become scary.

Instead of sitting on my hands with 100 shares of stock that could be trading at $35 a share, or worth $3,500, I now have 346 shares worth $12,110. That's how investors who learn the connection between the company, the customer and the cash register get rich.

The Third Step

Now that you know where you stand, each week check the value of your investments – the stocks and mutual funds in your personal account, your IRA, SEP-IRA, 401(k) or 403(b). As you already know, a group of us did this each Saturday morning at Starbucks and reviewed the end of the week numbers. It's not the cozy surroundings, or maybe the best food, but whatever it is we trade stories, catch up on the news, and drink coffee. And, I have to confess, we also think about how much money we're making for every customer who comes in the front door.

With the paper stock tables laid out on the counter each of us did the weekly 15-minute drill. We locked heads and went over the results. Who was down 5 percent from the recent high? John, who missed last week's meeting, was down 9 percent.

"Son of a gun," he wailed. "That missed meeting cost me a lot of money. But I know what you're going to say, I should have sold that sucker two weeks ago."

The group sat around and smiled. One regular, with a roll on his fork, took a gulp of coffee and said. "Well, fellows, for most people their plunging stocks don't bark, but thanks to our weekly meeting ours die before they bite."

Remember, like our group meeting at Starbucks, it's the numbers you're after. Keep a log of each security, its purchase price, current price and price trend.

You won't be able to buy and sell at just the right time, nor do you have to. And it's rarely worth spending an additional 90 percent of your time to get a one percent increase in performance. But I promise you'll feel a sense of relief as you watch other investors, who hang on in the eternal belief that in a plunging stock market the price will come roaring back, continue to lose money.

Again, for the record if the stock or fund has fallen more than 5 percent from its recent high, or 5 percent under your original purchase price, sell. If you read where the Dow Jones Industrial Averages took a big hit, you might want to check your holdings and sell mid-week. If you feel the stock or fund is in a forced sharp decline, you could sell immediately.

Above all, don't try to second guess the market.

> Most of the small investors I've
> known have gone to the poor house
> expecting the stock market to run
> in their favor if they just
> waited long enough.

Once you get the hang of managing your investments each week you can probably cut the loss on your stock and sell with less than a 5 percent dip in price, but you'll have to be careful of false bottoms.

The fourth step:

This is ultimately about having a plan to gain the ability to protect the value of your investments in a falling market by selling, and later using the cash to buy back your stocks to double your money in an up market.

Managing my money I look at the original investment as the starting point. As the months unfold I'm willing to lock in a profit even if the price goes higher later on. That's because, once the stock price trends downward you can't live on hope that it will rebound.

Once you sell the stock, put the money in your money-market or cash account. I call this holding place the Lock Box. Above all, don't worry about how much interest you'll earn. The important point is you want the money available when you buy the stock.

I believe this is one of the most important steps. By keeping the money intact you'll have the cash to make the instant buy on a stock at the beginning of the up market.

Kids can play this game!

I wanted to know if Trend Investing was easy enough for kids to master the concept. We sent out the material and to my radio producer's surprise on the line was Katie, a 14-year-old investor from Illinois, who said, "Got your stuff and every morning I grab the stock pages to see how my stocks are doing. My mom thinks it's great and she can't believe how much money I'm making. But I have one complaint," she sighed. "I now face a reduction in my allowance."

Another caller on the line was Chris, a 15-year old from Arizona. "How are you doing with the Trend Investing package we sent you?" I asked.

"Great," was his immediate reply. "I first had my money in a bank account and I didn't make much so I got some money from my dad and so far I've made $400 on paper. My dad wants to know how I do it!"

Now kids or adults can set up a personalized investment plan in which they can make the decisions and start to build their retirement plan.

Step 5:
Build Your Retirement Plan

You may remember the market crash of 1987, or, the market closing after the 9/11 attack. Or the mortgage crisis of 2008 which was followed in 2009 by the worst recession in decades that sent the stock indexes to their lowest level in 12 years. These were scary times indeed.

But with the recent stock market slide investors are increasingly looking for the next hot stock that's set to double in price in the next month. As a result, soothsaying has become a great cottage industry. Newspapers, magazines and television programs continually dance overnight riches in front of our eyes and sometimes we feel like a fool if we don't grab the latest opportunity to get rich.

But managing money and building your own retirement nest egg does not require reading a $200 a year investment advisory newsletter, or the opportunity to grab the 100 best stocks for just five bucks a week. Even as I write this book I opened my mail to another investment newsletter with large type I can't miss: This Tiny Biotech Stock Could Make You 405 percent Richer In the next 60 days.

Another newsletter tells me for $200 a year I can learn the name of a stock that can make me ten times richer this year and hand me a 1,000 percent profit.

Thank you for the tip, but I'll trust Mark Hulbert. In The Hulbert Financial Digest he tracks the performances of over 100 investment newsletter. He says of all the investment newsletters he tracks only a relatively few actually do better than the overall market.

Or, as I learned from the traders on Wall Street, throwing darts at a wall could give you better results than a financial hot-tip newsletter with unknown biotech stocks ready to explode. In fact, the Wall Street

Journal once had a weekly contest between several stock pickers from major brokerage firms and a staffer throwing darts at the paper's stock pages tacked up on the wall. Flinging the darts won most of the contests.

"It was too embarrassing to compete with darts," a friend told me. He agreed the newspaper should drop the contest.

And you also don't need to invest in mutual funds where the big-named portfolio manager wants you to believe he or she can outguess the stock market. Why? Peter Lynch, who set performance records year after year as the portfolio manager for Fidelity's Magellan fund, says trying to time the market is a waste of time. "I don't know anyone who has been right more than once in a row."

Recently a television commercial for a major stock broker pictured the bulls running up Wall Street in panic, yet the announcer asserted that with this firm's help you could not only avoid being trampled by the herd, but know which bull to ride to riches. There's only one problem with this ad. The real heard on Wall Street carries briefcases and they panic as often as the cattle.

With every broker recommendation I'm always reminded of the famous question asked at a resort where several stock brokers had moored their pleasure boats: Where are all the *customers' yachts?*

The good news is you don't have to be a financial wizard or out-guess the market to succeed in building a sizeable retirement nest egg. You just need to take charge of your investments, meet on Saturday morning and managing your money on a weekly basis. As a bonus, following these rules could even earn you a little cocktail *braggadocio* over your earnings.

Keep your plan simple

In your new retirement plan it's a good idea to limit your investment portfolio to just a few stocks you can follow each week with products you understand. Don't let a financial planner or broker design an investment plan that loads you up with several mutual funds and dozens of stocks of recommended picks with glowing recommendations from Wall Street analysts. You know the kind, where you find out later the *buy* recommendation wasn't a sure thing, and the *hold* should have been *sell*.

If you have $10,000 to invest, you could start with maybe four stocks. With $50,000 or more, your portfolio could include six stocks. Like most famous investors it's best to invest in just a few stocks so you can follow the company's sales and profits and learn how they affect the share price. I typically have six to eight common stocks in my entire portfolio.

But with only a few stocks you've got to be choosy and invest only in the bluest of blue chips. The thirty stocks that make up the Dow Jones Industrial Averages are usually some of the biggest names in America and owned by more investors than almost any other stock. In fact, I learned on Wall Street that the more investors who own a stock the more likely you are to make money on that stock.

Here are the important points in picking a stock:

Invest in a profitable company

The company must have a history of reporting strong earnings over a period of at least five years. It has more cash than long-term debt, and its profit margins are at or above the industry standards. Ideally, earnings growth should have accelerated in a rising economy since unprofitable companies or start ups do occasionally rocket up the charts, but don't bet on them.

Remember, for the most part, the price of a stock will follow its earning per share. In fact, if you lay a chart of the price of the stock over the past few years on top of a chart of the earnings per share, the lines will typically mirror each other. Earnings are also important when the stock market takes a dive. In those cases, the stocks with good earnings will typically fare better. As they say on Wall Street: A company that isn't making money for itself can't make money for investors.

Never invest in a regulated industry

Forget about telephone companies, energy companies, and airlines. They're often limited by regulations to what they can charge for their services. If they can't make a lot of money when the economy is strong you don't want to own the stock.

Invest in a long time market leader

You should be looking for well-established listed companies with strong customer demand for their products and therefore a clear lock on the market. It could be a unique product like Coca-Cola, Starbucks, or branches on every corner like Bank of America.

Invest in a well-known brand name.

The reason is that corporate brand familiarity helps attract buyers and builds profits. A study by a brand-strategy consultant Corporate Branding LLC found that in a ten year study of thirty-two companies those found to have the strongest brands had a return of 402 percent, compared with 309 percent for the Dow Jones Industrial Averages.

Invest in a company at least twenty years old

It takes at least twenty years for a company to establish itself and have a solid enough position in the industry to assure continued profits and growth. If you feel compelled to chase the latest new hot stock, consider what happened to investors in the last start up collapse.

From these painful reminders you can learn that it's better to come to the party late, or not at all.

Never buy a cheap stock

It's human nature to think that stocks you've been considering buying are now a bargain after the shares have plunged to new lows.

You're told the traffic light has turned from red to amber, and it's just the right time to step on the gas. But after a stock has taken a big dive the chances are the big institutional traders, pension and mutual fund managers have probably already slammed on the brakes, cut their losses and sold the stock. That could leave individual investors seeking a low price stock headed for a big-time crash.

I suggest the following approach:

Rule 1: Invest in hot companies with increasing profits and sales.

Rule 2: Sell as soon as the profits fall and the stock turns cold.

Rule 3: Buy back as soon as the profits and sales turn hot

This type of Investing requires you to not only recognize the start of an upward sales trend and a downward trend, but on the next economic recovery cycle the upward trend. In order to do this it's important to understand that **you are not picking stocks in the classic way.**

This strategy save a lot of time since you don't have to read about the hot stock picks or focus on operating margins, debt levels, and to identify the best investments.

You are looking for big blue-chip nationally known stocks that are actively traded on the major exchanges that will quickly react to an increase and decrease in sales and earnings.

Then find a company who is a leader in the industry. If you invest in a well-known company it's unlikely you'll wake up in a cold sweat when the stock takes a nose dive or bankruptcy is declared. You know the kind that I've used as examples in this book: General Electric, Starbucks, KB Homes, and Bank of America.

Need ideas for picking your next stock?

Why not take a trip to the local shopping mall and see what's new and popular? As you read the paper study what new products have appeared, what businesses are going to be affected by the economy, what new product you think will take off. Consider each item of interest a potential investing idea. Find out from the packaging the name of the manufacturer, then race to Google to see if the stock is listed and its history. You will know you are on to something when you find your friends want to buy one of the products you've discovered.

To find the right stock you are looking for the introduction of a new product like pantyhose that swept the competitors off the department store shelves. One of my best recent finds was Hansen Natural, a soft drink maker who discovered the health foods market and then launched the number two energy drink Monster. I watched sales soar as health food stores sprang up everywhere and company earnings took off like gangbusters. The share price rose several hundred percent until a downturn in the price of the stock occurred and I sold the stock.

Remember, sell when they turn cold, buy when they turn hot.

With the market madness on Wall Street it's a good time for a gut check to see how the weekly 15-minute drill has performed. The following examples do not include stock dividends, only the change in share price.

Here are some examples:

KB Homes

Once you've spotted the industry trend do your 15-minute a week drill. Watch the company stock. If you're right, customer demand for the product is rising and the industry is turning **hot.** You should see an increase in expected earnings and a spike in the price of the stock. That's just what happened to KB Homes. Once the stock was up 5 percent from the recent low it should confirm an upward trend. I didn't need to know anything else; I was locked in on the coming demand for homes because with ample credit the economy had made a comeback and consumer spending was running wild. You remember the days; home buyers were on a waiting list, paychecks were fatter and the good times were here.

At that time, when the real estate market was just starting to pick up and you could see home builders ramp up to meet the possible demand, I invested in KB Homes – one of the nation's largest home builders - buying the stock at $38 a share. Then in 2006, when builders could not build new homes fast enough to avoid a buyer's bidding war, I sold when everyone wanted to buy the hot home builder's stock at $82 a share. My original investment of 100 shares of stock was $3,800. My selling price of $82 a share made my 100 share investment now worth $8,200.

Again, reading the newspapers, I began to see signs of a cooling in the industry. Sales were slowing down, problems were developing with unsold homes, and stories appeared of possible problems in the future. Each week I reviewed my price logs and when the stock had risen 5 percent from its low, I repurchased the stock at $10 a share. Tight with money as I am, I used the amount of cash in the lock box from the previous KB home stock sale of $8,200, and bought 820 shares.

Here's a review of K B Homes:

January, 2005 buy 100 shares @ $38 for $3,800

January, 2006 sell 100 shares @ $82 for $8,200

March, 2009 buy 820 shares @ $10 for $8,200

March, 2010 hold 820 shares @ $17 at $13,940

By the spring of 2010, KB stock followed the housing recovery with a share price of $17.   With 820 shares the value was $13,940 against a buy-and-hold 100 shares with a value of $1,700.

Now if I have the patience to wait for the housing recovery and for buyers to go back on waiting lists, and if I pass up the hot stock tips and the mutual funds that often flame out, I can over time turn my original purchase of KB Homes stock into a gold mine.

For example, let's say the housing market recovers with buyers back on waiting lists in 2012, but the price of the stock is off its previous high of $82 and trades at $72 a share.

Then my last line would look like this:

June, 2012 hold 820 shares @ $72 at $59,040

My original purchase of 100 shares @ $38 was $3,800, but waiting for the housing recovery my holdings in 2012 might be $59,040. Not bad for a 7 year investment!

I like home builders because I know from time to time they will have a great demand for their product, and after the housing recovery runs its course the top of the market will again send their shares on a downward slide. I will be waiting.

Here's the important point:

Rule #7

It's not the money, it's the number
of shares you own that's important.

Wells Fargo Bank

One more case of a hot company turning cold was another bank too big to fail. In 2009 the government poured cash into the company and the stock market sent the shares into the dumps. But, I asked myself, if the company is too big to fail, how can it fail? It turned out it couldn't.

In October, 2007 I held 400 shares of Wells Fargo Bank stock. Reading the papers I could tell that declining home sales and falling prices could put a lot of homeowners at risk dropping the value of the bank's mortgage loan portfolio. I then sold at $35 a share when the sub-prime mortgage mess had begun to affect the bank stocks. The company was turning **cold.**

I put the $14,000 in the Lock Box and waited for the financial market to continue its spiral down. I watched the mortgage mess take the stock down to $ 10 a share by February, 2009. This was a historically low price for this stock. The fourth largest bank in the country was in good overall condition, but it had run out of cash. But with branches across America, it was in an excellent position to wait for an economic upturn. By March, 2009 –when no one wanted to buy the stock - my 15-minute drill told me it was time to buy at $8.60 a share. With the $14,000 of cash in the lock box I could buy 1630 shares.

Here's a review of Wells Fargo Bank:

October, 2007 sell 400 shares @ $35 for $14,000

March, 2009 buy 1630 shares @$8.60 for $14,000

March, 2010 hold 1630 shares @$30 at $48,900

My feeling was Wells Fargo Bank, with a solid customer base and branches all across America and integrating stock broker Wachovia into their branching system, should prosper as the economy recovers. The share price may not return to its former high of $40 a share, but the stock could return to at least $35 a share by sometime in 2012.

Then my last line would look like this:

March, 2012 hold 1630 shares @ $35 at $57,050

The bad news? The buy and hold investor, with the original 400 shares, could have an account worth $14,000.

I don't want to drive you crazy, but as one of my friends asked, "What are you going to do if the price of the stock goes back to its original high of $40 a share?"

As you might guess by now, I'm waiting. My account could then be worth $65,200. From $8.60 to $40 a share, that's the kind of numbers they like on the floor of the NYSE and I like in my pocketbook.

General Electric

This was a case of following the 15-minute a week drill and looking at the biggest company in America. I figured it was also too big to fail. The good news was I was following the smart big-time investors. One of the nation's largest companies, and one of the original 30 Dow stocks, GE shares had just closed at an 11-year low. This is one of my favorite stocks from the time I grew up in Omaha during the Great Depression. Like many long-time stock investors I wear my shoes and drive my cars long after most people would have traded them in. It's a habit of having money to invest in stocks, and if I'm right after all these years the General Electric stock should be back to its recent high of over $38 a share in a couple years. Even without collecting interest, that's a 60% return on my money.

With the 15-minute drill each week I was able to watch GE's big financial unit hit the turbulence of the big brokers and banks on Wall Street and take a hit on the price of GE stock The weekly numbers told me that by March, 2009 I should buy the stock at $7.06 a share. Again, I bought 400 shares for $2,824. By the end of 2009 the stock was around $17 a share. That's about a $10 per share gain and what I like is at least a one hundred to one hundred fifty percent increase from the original purchase price.

I know you probably don't want to read this, but the gang on Saturday morning who invested in GE stock could make a bundle when the economy recovers from the recent downturn. The profit from a buy price of $7.06 to $38 a share sometime in early 2012 is what the traders on the floor of the New York Stock Exchange call a good day's work.

Here's a review of General Electric

March, 2009 buy 400 shares @ $7.06 $2,824

January, 2010 hold 400 shares @ $17, $6,800

January 2012 hold 400 shares @ $38, $15,300

Office Depot

In a 15-minute a week drill with the gang at Starbucks we moved beyond our golf scores and the color of our grass and found Office Depot stock. One of the world's largest office product suppliers, the 2008-9 recession reduced business spending on office supplies and retail sales had fallen to a point where in March 2009 the stock was trading for $1.80 a share.

With that price we all piled into our cars and visited the local Office Depot store. We talked to the sales people, checked their expectations of customers returning once the economic recovery began and found the company was started in 1986. It had well-established retail store locations across America that could not be duplicated today at twice the cost. We decided that once the cash registers started ringing again we would make money.

Each Saturday we watched the price of the stock increase to $2.20 a share. Feeling confident we had the right numbers we made a big splash and each member of the Saturday morning gang bought 400 shares of the stock for $880. One year later, March, 2010, the share price was almost $8. Our original $880 investment had turned into $3,200.

Now we'll wait for the stock to return to its high a few years ago of $35 a share. It may take a couple of years, but this could be a very profitable wait.

Here's a review of Office Depot

March 2009 buy 400 shares @ $2.20 for $880

April 2010 hold 400 shares @ $8.00 at $3,200

April 2012 hold 400 shares @ $35.00 at $14,000

The important point in all of this is that you can build a huge retirement nest egg following just a few stocks. The problem is most people invest in stocks or funds with only a hope the share price will rise and then fail to watch them on a weekly basis. As a result:

Rule #8

Buy-and-hold investors can have half the account balance of an investor who sells when stocks go down and re-buys when stocks tend upward.

Again, the habit you need to develop is finding time each week to do the 15-minute drill. If you have to go to Starbucks each Saturday, do it! If you can build your own portfolio on your computer, update the files!

Then remember to keep a list of stocks you don't own but are tracking each week on a separate list.

Nationally-known stocks you think will benefit when business picks up in the coming months. If one of the stocks falls to historically low price when panic strikes the market, when everyone wants to bail out of their stock it could be a good time to buy.

From my 30-years experience on Wall Street, the stock price will come back and you'll almost always make money over time.

Step 6:
Be Aware Of The Time Clock

A letter from a reader tells this story. "My 23-year-old daughter recently started working and she is making payments into her stock fund from her paycheck each month until she reaches $10,000. Then she doesn't want to invest in the market anymore. She tells me she can let it mature until she turns age 65 and retires. Is that possible?"

My answer was simple. Based on what's happened to investments in the stock market over the past forty-two years I believe she could have a million dollars in the account when she retires. There are, of course, no guarantees, but even with inflation her retirement nest egg should enable her to retire in comfort without ever investing another dime.

I know several people who made regular contributions over the past 45-years to become some of the richest people in America. She may not do as well as Warren Buffett, who was offering shares of his new company Berkshire Hathaway for $12 ten years after I left college and found myself working on Wall Street.

But you can tell how well the time clock worked for Warren Buffett: Today, those $12 shares could be sold for over $100,000. In other words, 45 years later buying 10 shares for $120 is now worth over a million dollars.

Money and *Newsweek* magazines ran feature stories about Anne Scheiber and her use of the time clock. Though she worked as an auditor for the IRS, her investment strategy of saving a small amount each month is one that can be used by anyone. She started with a $5,000 investment in blue chip stocks in 1944 and over time let the clock build her nest egg to more than $22 million by the time she died in 1996. What struck me about Scheiber's story was her ability to overcome hardships, the persistence to continue investing and to keep her nest egg locked up until she retired.

Not a risk taker, Scheiber invested only in well-known companies that she found at the grocery store and at work. By continuing to invest in these blue-chip companies her annual return over time was a whopping 22.1 percent.

I know from radio callers and in my own life, and from taking to people across America, that ordinary people can accumulate extraordinary amounts of money if they follow a few basic rules, save a few dollars each month and watch the time clock. One such person was someone whom I admired, and who had built a fortune from investing small bits of money regularly over the years. I asked him what advice he could share that might help other investors.

"In a word: persistence," he said. "Just because everyone else follows the advice of what they see on television, or what they read in the papers or hear from a stock broker, doesn't mean that you shouldn't trust yourself. If I had one idea to give people who are striving to build wealth today on a tight budget, it would be let time and persistence work for you.

"What's more, the most profitable time you can spend is watching your stocks hit bottom, buying, and then watching the stock hit the top of the economic recovery and sell. Over time it has always worked for me.

"Take for example some of Wall Street's great bottoms. I remember clearly the stock market plunge in 1987 when I bought at the bottom of the crash. The second major bottom was in July 1996 when the Dow Industrials fell to around 5,400 and within a few months bounced back to more than 6,500. The last," he said with a smile, "was the March, 2009 market plunge to a Dow of 6,500 only later that year to snap back to over 10,000.

"But one last thing I'd like to share with you," he continued, "buying on the dip during those last three market meltdowns has accounting for most of my current wealth. The time spent watching when to buy near the bottom of the downturn, is the secret. That's where you make a great deal of your money, but very few individual investors realize that."

But the good news for everyone reading this book could be Rule #9:

Rule #9

What you make at work does not control what you can accumulate.

As I've already said, building wealth depends more on changing your spending habits and using the time clock than the size of your paycheck."

If you're a 20-something, the cost of financial security starting now with the clock in your favor is tiny, but even if you're a middle-ager facing a late-life financial security crisis, the cost can be well within your reach.

How do I know this time clock can bring you wealth on a few dollars a month? Because both *Time* and *USA Today* says it has worked.

The first American identified in print as a "millionaire," Pierre Lorilard in 1843, became rich because after he made his money his wealth multiplied many times over. Nor was this helping hand forgotten by the first person to be written up as a "billionaire," John D. Rockefeller in 1861. Yet today, most people fail to understand it was primarily through compounding over time that these men built the wealth that lives on today.

But as great as compounding is, it takes time to multiply the dollars. But them the numbers in your investment account can explode:

Had your grandfather invested just $100 in the Dow Jones Industrials in 1900, you would now have more than...
$70 million

An IRA for your grandkids

One of the best examples I know of explaining the tremendous power of compounding is for a grandparent or parent to open an IRA for a teenager. Assuming in the tax year the student has at least $2,000 of earned income from part time summer jobs, they can deposit this same amount in his or her IRA. If they start making the annual $2,000 contributions to the IRA at the student's age 19, and continue the annual contributions to his or her age 26 and the money earns a ten percent annual return, the IRA should be worth over one million dollars at age 65.

John D. Rockefeller hello........ One hundred fifty years later someone else figured out the magic of compounding. In this case, the parent or grandparent made a total of eight $2,000 annual contributions to the IRA, or $16,000 to provide a one million dollar surprise at retirement.

How does it work?

The magic of compounding is that each year your money earns money on the entire previous balance in your account and on any new contributions for that year. The really big secret is that as the years unfold, and the total amount in your account grows, then the more you automatically earn each year.

For example, here's how the money tree grows:

Year 1 $1,000 @ 9 percent return
End of year 1 account value $1,090
End of year 2 account value $1,188
End of year 3 account value $1,293
End of year 4 account value $1,409
End of year 5 account value $1,536

The "key" to compounding is without any additional contributions the initial $1,000 increased to $1,500 in just five years. Now let say it's your IRA and you contribute $1,000 each year at the beginning of the year.

A money tree with $1,000 annual contributions @ 9 percent return

End of year 1 account value $1,090
End of year 2 account value $2,278
End of year 3 account value $3,573
End of year 4 account value $4,985
End of year 5 account value $6,524
End of year 10 account value $16,560
End of year 15 account value $32,000
End of year 20 account value $55,765
End of year 25 account value $92,324
End of year 30 account value $148,575

Now you can begin to see how folks like Rockefeller built a vast fortune on the principal of compounding by taking a $30,000 initial investment and over time turning it into an account value of almost $150,000.

Another reason to be aware of the time clock is that under this example the IRA doubles its value between year 10 and 15 with only a $5,000 contribution. Then more than doubles again between year 15 and 20 and almost doubles again between year 20 and 25.

If you remember nothing else from
this book, burn this into your mind:
compounding is the most important
factor in accumulating money.

Another example of time and money:

Let's start by putting a penny on your dresser and each night thereafter on your way to bed you double the number of pennies on the dresser top. After ten days, you'd have $5.12. By continuing to double the number of pennies each night, you'd reach $163.84 by the fifteenth night. You still have lots of room on the top of your dresser and it might appear that nothing much will happen. But in just five more days you'd need a big dresser top. The pile of pennies would now total $10,485.76. In another five days the amount would have grown to $167,772.16. At the end of just the first thirty days the pile of pennies could take over your bedroom. You now have a total of $5,368,709.12. In just a few more days you'd have every penny in the country on your dresser top.

Design a retirement plan based on pennies.

The 1,000 Pennies-a-day Program

How can you get rich on just 1,000 pennies a day? The secret again is the magic of the power of compounding. Again, the really big secret is that as the years unfold, and the total amount in the account increases in value, the greater you automatically earn each year.

Now let's apply the compounding of a penny saved each day to your retirement savings plan. Assume you're 35 and have 30 years to collect Social Security checks. If you save 1,000 pennies a day [That's $3,650 yearly or about $300 a month in contributions] to your IRA over the next 30-years, and you earn a 9 percent annual return, you could have an IRA worth over half a million dollars!.

No, that's not a misprint. In this example you invested $3,650 each year for 30 years, or a total of $108,000. But, with the help of compounding your IRA has turned into a money machine. Now here's what gets scary. Your IRA now totals $555,000. Over the years that's an average annual gain of about $15,000 a year. You got it! You're taking $3,650 out of your paycheck each year, but on average, over the 30 year building period, you're increasing your nest egg over $15,000 each year.

If that doesn't wet your lips for more, here's another compounding secret. If you have enough spare cash to wait another five years after retirement to begin withdrawals from your IRA, you've hit the jackpot. Your investment account could then total about three-quarter of a million dollars.

The point of this lesson is that nothing much has changed in the game of building wealth. No matter how early in your life you start to invest, no matter how much money you earn, if you make regular contributions to a retirement plan you should build wealth the same way the bankers and brokers have done when I started on Wall Street.

Step 7:
Be Proactive And Never Give Up

Everyone loves a magic show. First you see it then you don't. Magicians create the illusion that what we thought we saw was real. I had a guest on the radio show who was both a stockbroker and a magician. He told me it's really all in the hands. Not that you need to be a magician to be a stockbroker, he said, but it never hurts. Before he came on the show, and without my knowledge, he put an ad in the classified section of the local newspaper that had my name and the three of hearts. On the air he asked me to draw a card from the deck and it was the three of hearts. He then showed me the ad in that day's paper. To this day I don't how he did it, but his sleight of hand was perfect.

Like the three of hearts, what I'm about to tell you may seem like it's from a magic act. You may have a strongbox full of stocks and mutual funds you've ignored and you're riding shotgun on a stagecoach going backward in time. If this dream applies to you; it's time to pull up the horses and get off the stagecoach.

Like millions of other individual investors you probably felt like hell when you witness a stock market meltdown and watched your investments shrink in value like an ice cube in the hot sun as you sat on the side lines waiting for the carnage to be over. That's because, after reading this book, your future success might depend on your courage to manage your own investments and to develop the habits necessary to build wealth.

Like the 15-minute drill each week charting the stocks you think will rebound from a market low or are about to top out when the economy starts to go into the tank.

Like anything else, something new can have troubling times. If you buy or sell at the wrong time don't give up. The good news is the basics of investing continue to work. Remember, you're not looking at the entire stock market or for the newest hot tech or computer stock that's set to take off. You're only working on, and investing in, maybe six or eight common stocks where you expect rising sales and profits or falling sales and losses – or you're keeping your cash in the lock box waiting for the next buying opportunity.

A big-time trader on Wall Street told my audience on the air that for most individual investors the stock market is like a man walking his dog.

"A successful investor is going from point A to point B by following a path of growing earnings. His dog is running off in different directions, chasing a rabbit, and barking at a squirrel. The smart man is too wise to wear himself out following the dog; he knows the dog and the stock market will be with him at point B. The difference," he said, "is he will have made money buying on the dip and again when the stocks went up, the dog will have been too busy chasing squirrels to avoid losing money when stocks go down."

As I talk with people who read the early copies of this book I learned they had found the courage to develop the habit of running the 15-minute drills each week, becoming more familiar with the stock charts in the newspapers, moving onto www.bigcharts.com, and then to online accounts with a discount broker which automatically displays the latest trends in their stocks.

As they gained more confidence in managing their money they tell me they now realize that what once held them in fear of the unknown was not as terrible as they had imagined. Now they feel on top of their game because with the magic of compounding whatever they save and invest each month could multiply by as much as nine or ten times when they retire.

Maybe you don't think this plan will work. But it's worked for professional investors, those I met working on Wall Street and for callers on my WOR radio program in New York and on ABC/KGO in San Francisco.

What's not too well known is traders who walk the floor of the New York Stock Exchange also watch the stocks and follow the downward and upward trend. They are close to the trading post so they can maybe gain a point or two from your weekly look at the stocks. But if you develop the habits outlined in this book, and have the persistence to work the numbers each week, you'll be closely following some of the biggest traders on the floor and learn why they make so much money year in and year out in an up and down stock market.

Remember, if you believe in the power of change, you can change the way you invest your money. And if you start right now, like thousands of other people who built sizeable retirement nest eggs over time, you'll find this change can lead you to a new and better financial life.

Most important of all, make up your mind you're going to adopt the habits of successful investors and manage your own money. I hope you find your dream of financial independence. I know you have every opportunity to do so.

Next, take these steps now:

First: To build a sizeable retirement nest egg you need to save for retirement with an absolute order of priority:

Make payroll deductions into the employer's plan to trigger the maximum company match program. Or, if your company does not have a matching program, sign up for payroll deductions into your own IRA or other individual retirement account.

Second: Open your own IRA and make as much of the allowable contributions as you can. Remember, a working spouse at home without taxable income can also participate in an IRA on the same basis as the employed spouse. Then remember the side bet: find out how you can add to your IRA or other personal savings account on a monthly basis. Sure, you don't have to make the IRA contributions until April 15 of the following year, or until you file your income taxes, but if you get in the habit of starting contributions in January you'll benefit from an additional 15 months of appreciation. Assuming you add $4,000 a year to your IRA at the start of the year you'll have earned about $26,000 in five years, only $18,000 by making the contribution just before tax time."

Third: Establish a time each week to review your stocks and investments with the *15 Minute Drill.* I've found this works best on Saturday morning when I can grab the papers for a weekly review of the stock market. But work something into your schedule that keeps you on target for the review each Saturday.

Fourth: Try to find a few friends to establish a Saturday Investing Club. Sometimes, over a cup of coffee, the decisions to buy or sell come easier when you're in a group. It's also fun to share new investment opportunities like Office Depot, were the group grabbed the stock for only $2 a share in March 2009 and in March, 2010 the stock had climbed to over $8 a share.

Thank you for reading this book!

About The Author

Jim Jorgensen has over thirty-five years experience in financial planning, as a broker on Wall Street and an investment consultant. He is the author of seven books on personal finance, including **The Graying of America**. His last book, **It's Never Too Late To Get Rich**, was published by Simon & Schuster.

He has been a radio host on WOR in New York City and ABC and CBS in San Francisco. For many years he was also a host of **Jorgensen On Money.**

Jim is a speaker at conventions and meetings and brings his down-to-earth study of investing on Wall Street, economic forecasts and his stories in the media from Washington and New York to audiences worldwide. He also provides employees with information on their company retirement and benefit plans and his clients often video his talk for employees in other locations.

He writes, with his son Richard Jorgensen, who covers technology from Silicon Valley, an electronic newsletter *The Financial Savvy Report,* imbedded with Podcasts of important developments of the week. For his clients, he also manages money based on what he learns from his early days on Wall Street.

He and his wife Nancy reside near Palm Springs California.

To keep you up to date on the latest ways to manage your money, your 401(k), IRA, Roth IRA and other investments, Jim Jorgensen wants you to receive a no-risk 3-week **free trial subscription** to his weekly e-newsletter:

The Financial Savvy Report

Your buyer's code is 4379

In this on-line report you can not only read the latest inside market investment and retirement news, but imbedded as Pod casts in the report you can listen to segments of Jim's radio program.

To receive your free trial subscription, send an e-mail with your name, address, buyer's code and comments on the book to:
Info@financialsavvy.com.

This book is also available as an ebook at Smashwords.com.

To learn how Jim Jorgensen can manage your money in his Trend Investing Portfolio, as outlined in this book, info@financialsavvy.com, or call 1-800-701-7283.

To book Jim Jorgensen as your next keynote speaker, check his schedule 1-925-209-7442.

Share Jim's wisdom with friends, family and colleagues...
To purchase additional copies of this book, visit Amazon.com.

The print version of this book is also available at special quantity discounts for bulk purchases for sales promotions, premiums, fund-raising, or educational use. Books can be created to fit special needs. Call 1-925-209-7442 for more information.